Between Artists

Between Artists

ANDREA BOWERS
CATHERINE OPIE

A.R.T. Press

ANDREA BOWERS in conversation with **CATHERINE OPIE**

Recorded at Catherine Opie's studio, South Central Los Angeles, June - October, 2007.

BOWERS: Maybe we should start by talking about the similarities in our histories?

OPIE: Our childhood?

BOWERS: Yes, exactly. I love how on the first night we met …

OPIE: At a cocktail party!

BOWERS: Right, at Miles Coolidge's house.

OPIE: Yes, that's where it was, at Miles and Amy's. That was when they were living outside of Valencia.

BOWERS: Just upon my graduation from CalArts in the summer of 1992, I believe.

OPIE: That night we discovered, to the horror and boredom of everybody around us, that we were from the same small town in Ohio.

BOWERS: Which is amazing! As I remember, the room was completely packed, and about an hour into our conversation about Ohio there was no one left in the room but you and me. *(laughs).*

OPIE: They couldn't care less about our shared history, but to us, all of a sudden, it became this major identifying moment. Two artists living in Los Angeles that grew up in the same small town that everybody only knows through the amusement park …

BOWERS: … Cedar Point.

OPIE: Cedar Point, in Sandusky, Ohio.

BOWERS: Right. I lived in the next town over, Huron. It's funny, both of us growing up in these little towns right on Lake Erie. Do you know that the area has grown tremendously since we left? It used to be farmlands, and now it's this kind of soulless sprawling suburbia. You and I saw the beginning of the era that transformed farmland into sprawling housing developments and WalMarts.

OPIE: Yes, it's true, kind of like what happened with the post-WWII suburban housing developments, but unlike those, the growth of our area was less about housing people for cheap and had more to do with farmers yielding their land because they couldn't make any money off of their crops. Fast forward twenty years from now and those same farmers will be upset because of a new era where America is trying to fuel itself through ethanol, making the price of corn increase to more than it's ever been in history.

BOWERS: So ironic. They would actually make more money now, or in the near future, off that land than they made from selling it to developers for those stupid housing developments. Now large corporations own most of the remaining farmlands. It takes 2,000 to 3,000 acres to make a living farming today.

OPIE: I know.

BOWERS: When we were growing up, the government was subsidizing the farmers. But they couldn't make enough money off of their crops to pay off their loans. I remember my grandfather diversifying his crops to soybean and leaving some of his fields unplanted. The banks held endless auctions due to farms going under because of the cost of technology, high interest rates and bad weather. My aunt, who worked in the farming industry her whole life, says you have to be an eternal optimist to be a farmer. You can still drive through central Ohio and see huge fields with old machinery left to rust. Because, you know, people just went broke. They started working in car factories.

OPIE: Yes, people turned to the new industry. But it's interesting because it looks like farming is going to take hold in this country in a way that it hasn't for many generations. So, who knows, maybe what will happen as the economy slowly dismantles is that, all of a sudden, bulldozers will be plowing over these master-plan communities *(laughs)* and bringing them back to farms! I've looked at, and of course despised, these abominations of the landscape for years. I've made work about them, not in Ohio, but in California. I moved to California when I was thirteen and I watched the same thing happen in California that you watched in Ohio, where the land became more useful as master-plan communities, rather than for farming.

BOWERS: You know they are selling ethanol at gas stations outside the Kroger's grocery store in Mechanicsburg, Ohio. *(laughs)*. My father, who still lives in the same house I grew up in, is pretty conservative. After the recent congressional elections, he told me that he and I could talk for more than five minutes again because he voted for a Democrat for the first time since Bush was elected. He's a real outdoorsman— he fishes and hunts. He makes his living as a commercial fisherman. Actually, I spent winters fishing in those icehouses you photographed. We called them ice shanties.

OPIE: Yeah, I grew up around them too. My grandfather also had an ice shanty. But when I went to photograph them in Minnesota for a project at the Walker Art Center in 2001, I decided to call them ice houses because they were like estates right there on the ice. They had satellite TV, little heaters, and specific architectural styles. You could even have a prostitute come visit you, or a pizza delivered *(laughs)* … it was really weird. The most interesting aspect of that series for me was trying to create landscapes about these temporary communities on the ice. They exist for just two months out of the year, but they are as complex and interesting as permanent communities. As everything becomes solidified, we have these temporary communities on the ice.

BOWERS: That's so interesting, a temporary community is such a potent political concept, one that I haven't really thought much about. I just make fun of *Burning Man* all the time. *(laughter).* It would be great if these ideas started to enter mainstream America. Thinking about the shifting landscape reminds me again of my father who has always been against environmentalism. For him it meant anti-gaming, but actually the gaming industry and environmentalism have some commonalities. Recently, for the first time, he voiced a concern for the amount of pollution caused by farming.

OPIE: Yes, with all the pesticides ...

BOWERS: It's the first time I've known my father to be concerned about the environment. I think I mention this because I see him as a bellwether for middle America. Maybe if his views are changing, then there is hope that we can do something about global warming. Perhaps an interest in protecting the environment is becoming an issue in mainstream America. Then again, I come from a tradition of "eternal optimists" ...

OPIE: Well, now Lake Erie is going through another huge crisis. They had cleaned it up, but all the fish are dying again.

BOWERS: I didn't know that.

OPIE: I saw a little article tucked in *The Los Angeles Times* about two weeks ago about how all the perch are on the shore again, just like they were when we were kids. It reminded me of the time when the Cuyahoga River was on fire. Lake Erie was completely polluted, and we grew up swimming in it.

BOWERS: It actually burned more than once, and so it was a real springboard for the environmental movement of the late 1960's. As a child my mother took me to the short, rocky Lake Erie beaches every day, but I remember many days when we weren't allowed to swim there because it was so polluted. The local paper would print announcements that you could not go into the water.

OPIE: Yeah, we both literally grew up in that lake, all summer long. Both of us were on swim teams, so it was either in the lake or in the pool, and that's how we spent our summers.

BOWERS: Our paths must have crossed. We were on competing swim teams, right?

OPIE: We swam against each other, I'm sure.

BOWERS: Can you talk about your surfer photos? Those portraits really take me back to my experiences as a swimmer. Did your childhood experiences influence that project?

OPIE: Probably—well, yes and no. As with the icehouses, I was thinking about the surfer photographs in relation to ideas of temporary community. I started making surf landscapes and then realized that I really missed making portraits. I hadn't made portraits since the *Domestic* series in '98. But there was also something else that kept happening with my work; everybody kept saying, "You know, every time you photograph people they're queer, but when you photograph the cities they're all empty," which in a way, was true. Making these very "real" portraits of surfers gave me a vehicle to explore portraiture outside of the queer community and to slightly change the direction of those possible interpretations of my work. Making the portraits made me think of my childhood, but they were also about this euphoria after surfing. My portraits are different from the iconic portraits of surfers though ... like, in mine, their eyes are all red, and they're spent. They're not the top surfers, they're just regular "guys." These images are reminiscent of childhood in that they are placed in the real. This is something that always comes back in my work—the idea of always placing things in the real.

BOWERS: When I see these surfer landscapes, I notice that all of these bodies of water that you're using in both California and Ohio have nuclear power plants sitting on their coastlines.

OPIE: Yeah, the Davis Besse Nuclear Power Plant sits right on the waterfront.

BOWERS: It always frightens me to see that power plant on the shoreline. It seems like an ominous disaster in the making. It will be interesting to see what happens to the area where we grew up because water is becoming a rare commodity, and they have a lot of fresh water. The Bush administration sees nuclear energy as the solution to climate problems and the democrats are being manipulated by nuclear energy lobbyists. Have we forgotten all the important work of the anti-nuclear activists in the 1980s? I made an entire body of work about these activists in 2003 called *Magical Politics*.[3] They were various alliances of women's groups. They really changed our thinking about nuclear power but their actions are so under-recorded. I want to go back to something you just brought up that caught my attention, "the real." In both of our practices, we advocate for documentary, what that process entails and how it can be used. An important part of my work is rediscovering and recording undocumented histories, so it's important to me to use archival processes for documentation, in order to retain these otherwise suppressed histories.

OPIE: Yes, it's like you create another kind of document within the work ... a document of a document. For you, is it also a way of investigating the real?

BOWERS: I feel like there is so much information left out of historical recording, or the recording of history—that what's recorded ends up only benefiting those in power—so I'm looking for what could be called a more real, or a more layered, documentation of what has happened historically.

OPIE: Both of us are trying to deal with history, but my approach is the documentation of people or places in the world. My work makes an archive, but your work begins in the archive.

BOWERS: I believe I do both. I am recording the histories of the activists I work with and I am documenting the significance of their input in relation to historical events.

OPIE: Are you an avid newspaper reader like me?

BOWERS: I read *The Los Angeles Times*, not *The New York Times*. Do you read both?

OPIE: No, I read *The Los Angeles Times* everyday. I might peek at *The New York Times* every once in while online, but I like the local news. I'm interested in the local community base, so I like to find out about things that I would never see in *The New York Times*.

BOWERS: I get all the ideas for my art from the newspaper. *(laughs)*. That's one reason I'm so concerned about the corporate take-over of locally owned papers and radio. The future quality of *The Los Angeles Times* is in doubt with the recent ownership. The paper's funding has been cut, in particular in the areas of investigative reporting. There have been so many high profile resignations.

OPIE: Rupert Murdoch has successfully taken on a whole new conglomerate of newspapers and other medias.

BOWERS: Yeah, this is a national trend that reflects the loss of diversity and freedom in the press.

OPIE: And all of this has changed so much from when we were growing up ... probably both of us were reading *The Sandusky Register*—did you read it?

BOWERS: Of course!

                (laughter)

OPIE: The other thing about where we grew up, and its effect on my practice, is the landscape—in a weird way. As a kid growing up, there was always a cornfield across the street from me. I mean, literally, there was never not a cornfield across the street from where I lived. I think a lot about Ohio, and ideas of landscape, and what it means to think about democracy and landscape together. Those hours I spent lying in the middle of a cornfield on my back looking up at the Ohio sky gave me many creative approaches to thinking out of the box. I guess I have this personal philosophy that comes from having an empty cornfield to stare into, as if the emptiness of it provides a blank slate to project onto.

BOWERS: Maybe that's part of why I leave so much negative space in my drawings—"a blank slate to project onto."

OPIE: I think a huge problem today is that there aren't empty spaces like this in our lives. Everything is so mediated; there is no space for the kind of critical thinking that so often has to come out of nothingness. And you know, it's funny, because Ohio has so much open space, but despite that, Ohio is a conservative state.

BOWERS: Although it also has a really strong union history.

OPIE: And there were all the underground railroads through

Sandusky too, all those houses with hidden chambers.

BOWERS: Yes, the safe houses throughout the state in the 1800s. Reaching Ohio meant reaching freedom, and hope for a better life for thousands of African Americans.

OPIE: That history was discussed a lot in my youth. Though of course, there was also an enormous amount of racism at that time.

BOWERS: Right. This has always been such an intense contradiction within the cultural fiber of Middle America. I was raised in a community with a strong and healthy emotional attachment to others (I like to call it emotional intelligence—something rare in the art world), and a commitment to community and family. People really took care of one another. Simultaneously, however, there was an embedded tradition of racism and sexism in the community. The need to respond to this dialectic has been a constant influence in my work. It's as if this protection of family and community leads to fear and hatred of strangers and foreigners, or anything that seems different. Patriotism tends to affirm those in power and stunt dissent. This is one of the main problems with patriotism, and there is a lot of patriotism in Ohio.

OPIE: That's true, and there wasn't any sense—or even talk—of feminism, even though we grew up at the time that feminism was taking off! You know, I was born in sixty-one, you in sixty ...

BOWERS: … sixty-five …

OPIE: … at that time the country was becoming radicalized to a certain extent. But the only memory I have of anything that I felt was radical was watching the evening news during the Vietnam War and seeing all the soldiers' names who had died that day scroll across the blue screen.

BOWERS: Yeah, I remember that too …

OPIE: The names of all the people we had lost in our community were on that screen. The scrolling of these names was literally a moment where we could mourn these losses.

BOWERS: It's that same sense of projecting into the void.

OPIE: Exactly, it's interesting, and curious too, because what we're talking about goes back to the notion of being grounded in a certain specific location, or landscape.

BOWERS: I think there is something that we both got from growing up in a small town in Ohio, like being able to put things in perspective. I've always leaned toward making work about local issues; there are so many nuances about a place that can only be understood from living within the community. However, I sense that the global art market discourages this approach. In *One Place After Another: Site-specific Art and Locational Identity*, Miwon Kwon wrote that, "The increasing institutional interest in current site-oriented practices that mobilize the site as a discursive

narrative is demanding intensive physical mobilization of the artist to create works in various cities
throughout the cosmopolitan art world ... There
follow repeated visits to or extended stays at the
site; research into the particularities of the institution and/or the city within which it is located ... and
many meetings with curators, educators and admin-
istrative support staff ..."[1] I wonder if these meetings and visits allow the artist to really understand
the local issues. It seems that, for example, many
of these biennials provide for only one research trip
prior to the exhibition. I seriously doubt that this is
enough immersion in the local community to avoid
the possibility of making work that comes unnerv-
ingly close to tourism or exoticism.

OPIE: Well, that's something that perhaps happens in my
body of work about American cities. I'm often afraid
that I am going to disappoint the local communities
with my vision, that I am going to somehow create
a history that they can't embrace. I find it very tricky
and a very scary thing. But so far everybody has
gone along with them. Nobody's ever come up to me
and said, "I can't believe the way you photographed
Chicago!" *(laughs)*.

BOWERS: But I think there is also a really important perspective that can come from being an outsider. I feel that
it's the people who live in a community that best
understand an issue or a situation, but local issues
are also global issues, so sometimes an outsider

1   Miwon Kwon, *One Place After Another: Site-specific Art and Locational Identity* (Cambridge, Mass: MIT Press, 2002), p. 46.

can bring a new perspective. That's my conflict and that's why I am also obsessed with research. I want to know everything I can about the communities I make projects about, and I feel like my work reaches out in some way. Your *American Cities Project* reminds me of this; I see it as a research project to create an archive of a community. Is that the case for you?

OPIE: The act of documenting does, in itself, create and archive, but there's also this underlying sense of economy that prevails in that history of looking at the specificity of location. The location I choose to photograph, be it Wall Street, St. Louis, Pittsburgh, or the downtown of Minneapolis, creates an economic examination on how cities function in America. All of it is about a shared economy. St. Louis wanted to be the grandiose city; Chicago was the working man's city. St. Louis wanted to be the gateway to the west, but Chicago completely surpassed them. And then there's Wall Street, one of the most powerful economies in the world in a very small area of land. That body of work changed entirely when the World Trade Center Towers came down. That's what happens with work, you never know how history will change the way it is read.

BOWERS: The turning point in my philosophy and art practice came when I was reading about Marxist and Situationist theories in grad school. For me, it was a huge realization to discover that I had been under the influence of a hegemonic system for most of my life.

OPIE: Mmm-hmm.

BOWERS: I grew up under the reign of so many unspoken rules that I was meant to follow, and these rules became normalized and passed down through generations. Once I realized I was under that kind of control, I was able take this sense of community and turn it into a more productive citizenry. Maybe, or at least I'm trying. *(laughs).*

OPIE: Well, that's an interesting thing, because Ohio has a very strong religious center, and religion is another type of community. My father was an atheist so I grew up being told that God didn't exist, which was really …

BOWERS: … totally unheard of in that part of the world. That's kind of cool.

OPIE: We weren't allowed to tell my grandparents. They were hard-core Baptists so, you know …

BOWERS: … yeah, that's amazing. From a very early age I didn't want to be involved in religion, but I remember feeling inferior because I wasn't Catholic. I felt left out of the ritual. Recently, maybe five years ago, I told one of my relatives that I was an atheist—not thinking it was a big deal—and my uncle in Ohio accused me of being a hedonist. *(laughs).* Some relatives were unsure if they wanted their kids around me.

OPIE: Yeah. That happened to me with my niece.

BOWERS: Really?

OPIE: Because I was a lesbian … because I was weird … and it's against the Christian faith. And after I made *Self-Portrait/Pervert* (1994), I was only supposed to be around my niece—who adores me—with adult supervision. I'm the biggest pro-kid person you could ever imagine. It was devastating; it was like everything fell apart for me then.

BOWERS: You're such an amazing mom. I can't imagine how horrible that must have been for you.

OPIE: Yeah.

BOWERS: I remember when we first met—it was around the time of the *Pervert* image—everybody would describe you as the biggest badass. People saw the work and were afraid of you. You were seen as so radical.

OPIE: I know. People were so scared of me. It was shocking to me. Reporters would come and interview me, and then afterwards be like, "You're really nice!" *(AB laughs).* And I'd say, "Well … yeah. What did you think?" I also remember offering, as a gift, to do portraits of the children of some prominent L.A. collectors who had an enormous amount of my work. And they said something like, "Well, you're not going to cut them or put needles in them are you?"

(laughter)

BOWERS: With all of the alienation and prejudice you have experienced, how do you come to terms with the notion of community?

OPIE: That's a hard question. The notion of community is complex to me because I have many communities in my life. I have the queer community, the art community, and then there's my own neighborhood that I am involved in. Within that there is always going to be potential for prejudice and alienation, but by creating these really beautiful images, I am trying to turn these prejudices around. I use the seduction of beauty to allow people to have access to, and look at, things that go beyond their own fears. I want to do this especially with the *In and Around Home* series, where I try to merge all these communities together. And I also try to be as sincere as possible. Both of us come up with those issues in our work.

BOWERS: Exactly. I use the same strategies of beauty, sincerity, and community in my own work. In the *Nothing is Neutral* project (2006), which included the video *Letters to an Army of Three*, I wanted to use aesthetics to seduce people into reconsidering their positions on the subject of abortion rights, which is no easy thing.[8] People's religious convictions tend to cloud their judgment around this issue, so it was a difficult subject to negotiate in my work.

OPIE: This relationship between ideas of politics, morality and ethics is interesting. We're both atheist, and yet we come out of this religious culture where the notion of community is directly related to church.

BOWERS: That's true, especially with the farm churches.

OPIE: I was thinking more about the Quakers or the Amish who create a kind of religious community that is also responsible to the earth, in terms of sustainability.

BOWERS: Well, I love the Quakers. I was born in a Quaker community. Perhaps, after all, there are some positive secular notions of community that can be recuperated from the church. The irony of my secularism is that I am constantly referencing the role of religion in protest—nonviolent civil disobedient protest —throughout my work. I'm about to go to Chicago to shoot a project at the Adalberto United Methodist Church in Humbolt Park—the Puerto Rican neighborhood. This small storefront church has given sanctuary to a young mother and her son. The mother, Elvira Arellano, is an undocumented immigrant and her nine-year-old son son, Saul, is an American citizen. She has been 'deported' but refuses to return to Mexico because she will not leave behind the child that she raised by herself. Saul's citizenship entitles him to stay in this country, and having spent his whole life in the United States, he really doesn't want to leave.

OPIE: Oh yeah, I know this story.

BOWERS: The two activists supporting Elvira Arellano's sanctuary are Reverend Walter Coleman and his wife Emma Lozano. They have a long history of activism. I just wonder if he became a pastor because he saw the church as a type of "free space" that gives a bit of distance from the government's involvement. Also the religious conviction of the congregation makes them more committed to their political actions. The institutional 'free space' of churches has given rise not only to democratic movements like Abolition, Catholic Workers, the Quakers and the Civil Rights Movement, but also the Klu Klux Klan, American Nazi Party and the New Right. I have only focused on the left-wing churches, and have great respect for what they have accomplished.

OPIE: Can you describe what you think a left-wing church is about?

BOWERS: I think it's a bit of a false dichotomy—this idea of a left-wing or progressive church. I'm not a believer and by no means an expert, but from what I know of Jesus's teachings, I think any Christian church should, by definition, be what we call progressive or politically 'left.' So it's the right wing, and the con-servatives' attacks on groups promoting tolerance and the work for peace and justice, that have cre-ated the idea that these goals are somehow leftist, rather than Christian. I don't know of anywhere in the bible that encourages people to practice hatred and intolerance. However, the dichotomy seems to exist in our current political climate; I see one group of religion supporting freedom, and another group organizing to eliminate individual freedoms.

OPIE: It's also interesting because freedom—just like "hatred," and "God", and "truth"—is a big, complex term that gets thrown around in relationship to the notion of democracy in our society. I mean, I feel like we all know at this point that democracy is a falsified freedom. It only exists within ideas that you have to swim through, negotiate, depending on that right-left issue, which I don't think has ever been as polarized as now. Everything is always under the guise of democracy and freedom, but the right has significantly changed the rules because of a religious fundamentalism. I don't know if they have changed the definitions of those words, but they have changed the playing field on which we have to think about them.

BOWERS: I know that our democratic system has been, and continues to be, eroded, but I really believe it is crucial to fight for the restoration and implementation of individual freedoms and human rights.

OPIE: Yeah, you have to.

BOWERS: And, you know, I believe we have a responsibility to other people and to allowing people to have differences.

OPIE: Have you ever seen the documentary *Jesus Camp*? It blew me away—and scared me terribly. It's a documentary about an evangelical Christian woman and a camp she runs in Devil's Lake, N.D. called *Kids on Fire*.

BOWERS: Is that the one that shows a church where the congregation prays in front of a life size cardboard cutout of George Bush?

OPIE: Yeah. There's a part where they have an abortionist come in with little tiny fetuses and the kids have to hold them and cry. Their idea is that if you get into these young minds as they are forming, these kids are going to become strong believers and be the next wave of crusaders. And to me that is just so sick. Imagine if the kids were being taught that only homosexuality was the right thing. *(laughs)*. You know that camp would be shut down by the government immediately.

BOWERS: Yeah.

OPIE: You can brainwash kids so easily—they are so receptive. I was so upset by that film that I actually had a hard time sleeping for four nights. I kept imagining my little five-and-a-half-year-old sitting there, listening to these absolutely insane people try to brainwash him.

BOWERS: Yes, it's insane. These people are spreading ideologies and doing it in really manipulative ways ...

OPIE: ... ways that can also change laws.

BOWERS: It frightens me to death because the real impact of this type of brainwashing will show up in the future. It's so scary. For a brief moment during the '60s and '70s, the Civil Rights Movement, the Women's Movement and the Peace Movement all insisted upon freedom and the eradication of social injustice. You and I benefited from these movements, but now we're at a point where we're going backwards.

OPIE: Really far backwards. It goes back to this idea of ethics and morality, in that many on the right truly believe that what they're doing constitutionally to human rights is honoring a Christian obligation to make the world 'better.' It's an intense belief system, but it's all tied up in this kind of overwrought Viagra moment of capitalism, you know? It's like capitalism was given a Viagra pill, and it stays harder than it ever could. *(laughs).*

BOWERS: Nice metaphor.

(laughter)

OPIE: Well, it's all about dicks anyway. *(laughs).*

BOWERS: Yeah, but it's of course just a few making as much money as possible and using xenophobia as a marketing tool. Do you think you've become more political with the reign of the Bush Administration and the fact that we're in this horrible war? How has the current political climate affected your work?

OPIE: Well, I think that's a really good question. I think that the biggest issue that I struggle with is how to continually keep my ideas, and work, honest, while keeping the work compelling both on an intellectual and visual level.

BOWERS: How do you define honesty in your work? And how do you get students to understand that?

OPIE: What I mean by that is to be honest with oneself in relationship to one's ideas and the pursuit of those ideas, paying attention to what you are passionately engaged with rather than to what the market may or may not want to see. Unfortunately, it is very difficult to get students to understand this because, as incredible as it sounds, at this point there's a big cultural difference between you and I and the people that we're teaching.

BOWERS: In what way?

OPIE: I have been teaching for fifteen years and I have watched the student body move through a number of cycles. We had really conservative students coming out of the first Reagan/Bush administrations that were really far on the right. To try to talk to them about abortion or human rights, and well, you can imagine how that might go. I have even had students at UCLA saying that the reason they are making art is for God. I don't know how to respond to that. I kinda want to say something like, "Well I hope God really likes it."

(laughter)

And now we're getting students that came out of the Clinton generation, and I find that those students are making work with much bigger political statements in relationship to politics under the current Bush administration. I'm not sure that this answered your question ... But let's go back for a minute, how do you make work that's political?

BOWERS: All artwork has a political agenda. I completely agree with what Adrian Piper said, "Implicitly political art reinforces unregulated free-market capitalism. Explicitly political art subverts the power relations that under gird it." Recently I went to a conversation at LAXART between Malik Gaines and Charles Gaines.

Charles's talk reminded me that art history permits certain philosophical issues in its domain but pure 'politics' isn't acceptable. He explained that the idea of politics is treated as being outside of art because it concerns itself with localized issues and not universalist philosophies. But he sees this as incorrect because specific social problems are not the only critical aspect of political discourse. The influence of philosophical ideologies on political policy is clear, and is inherent in all debate. I think I'm evolving into a more explicitly political artist. What about you?

OPIE: I was more political early on, when I was at San Francisco Art Institute. Angela Davis was my 20th-century philosophy teacher. The war in El Salvador was going on and it was during the Reagan Administration. One of the best things about living in San Francisco is that it's one of the most leftist political communities in this country. And it's the perfect place to come out as a young lesbian. I mean, I was in heaven. I was constantly taking to the streets. I was in every protest, and I have all those protests documented. I have images of the first march when Jesse Jackson gave a speech—all the gays and lesbians took to the streets to go down and support Jackson. And then AIDS happened, and that was the end of feeling a sense of wholeness within the community.

BOWERS: But that was the center of protest, the Castro.

OPIE: Right, the community became polarized between "us and them." I photographed the first candlelight-vigil march for AIDS. It was in the Castro and I was watching so many of my friends die. And it was before the cocktail or anything, you know? And I actually worked on the AIDS Memorial quilt—which you have just made a series of works about.

BOWERS: Yes. *The Weight of Relevance.*

OPIE: I worked in San Francisco sewing quilts together. I was a horrible sewer in those days. They had me fold.

(laughter)

BOWERS: They had you fold?

OPIE: It turned out that I couldn't really sew. Even though I wanted to sew, I couldn't really sew, so I was folding.

BOWERS: Imagine all the folding and mending now! That was twenty years ago. The quilt, which memorializes the names of loved ones who have died from AIDS, now weighs 54 tons and still there is no cure for the disease. The demographics have changed and now the highest percentages of people contracting the disease are young people, women, and people of color.

OPIE: Yeah, the demographics have changed. It started as an issue within the gay and lesbian community and became a large grass roots political movement like the Civil Rights Movement and the Peace Movement. The black community needs to do some of what the gay and lesbian community did to bring awareness back to this issue. It's a shame, because AIDS has now been with us for over 22 years and there is no longer a political mobilization about it in America.

BOWERS: In Africa yes, but here, no.

OPIE: I wonder what Angela Davis would have to say about this. Did she ever write about this?

BOWERS: I don't know.

OPIE: It all changed for me when I moved to Valencia to go to CalArts. At age thirteen, I had moved from Ohio to Rancho Bernardo, a master-plan community of Southern California, and then all of a sudden I moved to San Francisco. It really helped me to have San Francisco as this political base from which to work. And then when I went to CalArts, here I was in Valencia, stuck in the master-planned community again.

BOWERS: At the time that you and I were both at CalArts ...

OPIE: Yeah. I graduated in '88.

BOWERS: ... I graduated in '92. At that time it was rumored that the head of the KKK was living in Valencia.

OPIE: And all the L.A. Police Department—like the Rampart division—because they didn't want to live in LA.

BOWERS: However, CalArts was this radical little bubble in the middle of it all.

OPIE: Exactly.

BOWERS: CalArts is a really close community. You live with each other—eat, sleep, party, make art and think.

OPIE: And have really, really interesting and radical professors.

BOWERS: We were bunkered in this little enclave in an extremely conservative community. I was studying Anarchism, Marxism, Feminism, the Situationists, gender politics, etc. My two years at CalArts changed my life and I formed life-long bonds with people. It's the Hotel California—"you can check out any time you like, but you can never leave."

OPIE: The people that I got to study with at CalArts were just as amazing as the people that I got to study with at The Art Institute. I mean, you had Douglas Crimp talking about AIDS for the first time; you had John Greyson, who was this radical young video maker. You had Gary Kibbens—you know, it was just amazing.

BOWERS: For me Lane Relyea, Charles Gaines and Millie Wilson were important teachers. Did you study with Allan Sekula?

OPIE: Allan, Catherine Lord and Millie too. And for me it was so interesting because I went from this San Francisco leather community to CalArts. Even though there was a queer presence at CalArts, it wasn't the same as the radical community that I had just left. And then I started photographing suburbia. Everybody kept saying, "Well, why aren't you making queer work?" and I kept saying, "this is queer work."

You have to make work about the norm to understand the notion of the norm and to begin to create a critical analysis of it. And it was the perfect place for me to try to reposition myself as a documentary photographer and a street photographer. It allowed me to shift the work towards a wider read than what I was doing before. Just photographing people doing SM in their houses wasn't enough for me. It wasn't interesting enough. It was just showing something without creating a dialogue.

BOWERS: Right. It can become about exoticism and objectification rather than about real people with identities and political positions and emotional connections, and all of those things.

OPIE: Can I segue at this moment ... you just said "real people," and it made me think about your use of photorealism.

BOWERS: Right. Well, the process personalizes the subject matter.

OPIE: But it also makes it more real. Don't you think that's what personalizing does ... it makes it real?

BOWERS: Yeah. For me it's about internalization, maybe even empathy. Monica Bonvicini (we met at CalArts as well) forced this idea out of me one night. We screamed at each other for about two hours in my kitchen because she cannot understand why I make photorealist drawings. I think the labor seems oppressive to her.

OPIE: Mmm-hmm.

BOWERS: Of course there are many philosophical and art historical reasons for using this style. But through the process of our debate, it finally hit me. As a child, I had a hard time with comprehension and retention of information; I'm a slow reader. In order to study I copied everything. I rewrote everything by hand and that was the only way I could learn the material. The content became personal. Still, to this day, it's the process I use to digest information.

OPIE: And disseminate the information.

BOWERS: As a child, it made sense to me to physically go through the process of recording information in order to be able to understand and recall it. Now, when I record these images or texts with my labor and craft, it becomes a part of me, and I understand it in a way that I can't understand just by looking or reading. I believe this digestion of the subject matter then transfers to a more personal understanding of the content for the viewer as well.

OPIE: It's interesting, because your process is similar to how we create memory. This somehow reminds me of a review I read of this really interesting book about the architecture of war.

BOWERS: How so?

OPIE: Because it made me think about private and public in the same way that our work reflects on ideas of private and public. The article was relating concepts of modernity to the technologies developed during World War II and the changes brought to domesticity and consumer culture by the production of these new materials.

BOWERS: These are ideas that are percolating.

OPIE: I mean, new technology creates a different kind of access to materiality that, obviously, can be used by the evildoers. *(laughter).* But it's interesting. I mean, for instance, behind you, in my studio, is an image of *The Hall of Architecture* in Pittsburg and it's going to be a hundred years old soon. Andrew Carnegie had a whole lot of buildings cast and installed them in *The Hall of Architecture* at The Carnegie so that the workers in the community would get to know the great pieces of architecture in history, and throughout the world. Meanwhile, all the steel mills have shut down in Pittsburgh and most of the steelworkers have become cabdrivers.

BOWERS: I can't help but think of Emma Goldman when I hear you talk about Andrew Carnegie as they were both alive during the turn of the century. The same exact time Carnegie's amassing his *Hall of Architecture*, this amazing Anarchist feminist Emma Goldman is lecturing, publishing and protesting for human rights—often speaking out for the rights of workers in particular. She was so often arrested that every time she spoke in public she carried a book to read in jail. She was born into a poor family, worked in sewing factories and gave every penny she made to her political causes. Just last year I finished a video installation that is a reading of the Emma Goldman text called *Marriage and Love*, published in 1910—also coming upon its 100 year anniversary. In this piece called *Vows*, two women in full wedding attire face each other and appear to be listening and responding, as though reciting marriage vows. I chose this text, which analyzes how the social institution of marriage is an oppressive institution of capitalism and oppositional to love, because many parts of the essay sound as though they were written last month *(laughs)*.

How did you decide to focus on the *Hall of Architecture*?

OPIE: It goes back to the history of labor in the United States. It's like how company towns have been created to supposedly sustain the worker, but really are keeping the worker working for the companies. "We're giving these beautiful buildings to you, so you never have to dream about leaving." *(laughs)*. But it's just, you know, it's ironic.

BOWERS: How will this irony be revealed in your photographs?

OPIE: Well the black and white panoramas will focus on the sites where the steel mills were—some of which are now abandoned and some of which have been transformed into malls. And then I will do the hall of architecture in color. Through the museum, the hall of architecture can stand and be preserved, but the steel mills were not preserved, nor were the jobs of the workers.

BOWERS: Yeah … But that's where hegemony comes in.

It takes a long time for the power structures to be revealed and there's so much fear on the part of the proletariat to deal with.

OPIE: Well, it's all based on fear.

BOWERS: And lack of education. "No child left behind."

OPIE: Yeah. And every child left behind. Religion becomes the source of education, which creates the fear.

BOWERS: Well, you know, you suffer in this life for a better life in the afterlife *(laughs)*. So, I wanted to get back to the apparent pluralism of your subject matter—for instance, how do you connect your photos of radical subcultures, with the work about suburbia—and the difficulties people had reading this pluralism.

OPIE: I think it's more that they questioned supporting pluralism. People thought that I should be making radical work about the queer community. I don't call myself a queer artist. But I'm also proud of being queer and adding to the visual dictionary of our community. I'm glad and proud to be a part of that culture. So I will call myself a "queer artist" in *that* way. But I also think it's just as important to photograph immigration marches or peace marches. If you really want to talk about democracy, it can't be considered under the guise of a singular notion of community; it has to be represented in the kind of multifaceted layers that actually exist within our world. I do not exist only in a queer culture—I exist in this world. And so I have to look at the United States in this broader way that I have been doing—through American cities, or documenting L.A., or looking at temporary communities of icehouses or surfers. To me, it's about trying to create a true democratic voice in relationship to my ideas about how I participate within American culture.

BOWERS: Yeah, likewise, I can give you a hundred different words that describe me and they still don't define me. One of my goals as an artist was to take ownership of those definitions, investigate the complexities, and not worry. I don't know how so many young people can refuse to be called a feminist. At this point I'm sick of that position.

OPIE: Yeah. That's why I call myself a feminist and a slut! *(laughter)* I might not be a feminist bitch, but I am a feminist slut. *(laughs).* But no, that's the thing, they feel that the feminist title has to be all-encompassing.

BOWERS: But feminism is multilayered by definition. I have this great old paperback that I go to every time I sense I'm banging my head on that glass ceiling. It's called *Woman Power* and the first page states that (I have it memorized), "Radical feminism is working for the eradication of domination and elitism in all human relationships. This would make self-determination the ultimate good and require the downfall of society as we know it today."[2] What young artist, or young student for that matter, would disagree with that?

---

2 Cellestine Ware, *Woman Power; The Movement for Women's Liberation* (New York: Tower Publications, Inc, 1970)

OPIE: But don't you think, also, that they're afraid of labeling themselves as a feminist because they think that it's a title for being a lesbian?

BOWERS: Oh shit, that's a painful thought. I thought you were going to say something else. (Pause) Well, I think it comes out of the right-wing backlash against feminism. Pat Robertson said, "Feminism encourages women to leave their husbands, kill their children, practice witchcraft, destroy capitalism, and become lesbian."

OPIE: What did you think I was gonna say?

BOWERS: Okay, here it comes. I thought you were going to say that young artists don't like to call themselves feminists because they think it will hurt the marketability of their work.

OPIE: Oh, my God. Actually, that wouldn't even pop into my mind.

BOWERS: I was just trying to think … who is more cynical, you or me? *(laughs).* Even the young artists who are critical of the market are struggling with its control over them.

OPIE: They're into marketing. Well, also, they're influenced by the marketplace's support of a particular kind of work by women, and a lot of that work that has influenced them comes out of the very male-dominated Yale Photography Program. I mean, when you look at the Katy Grannans and the Justine Kurlands and the Anna Gaskells … the work is about the vacant woman. And then you have all the younger women who've used their sexuality. ... Daphne Fitzpatrick and I sat in on a conversation in New York—we were like these two butch dykes sitting there with all these women with their boobs falling out of their dresses talking about trying to create a feminist position in their work. Daphne and I just left shaking our heads going, "They have absolutely no clue!" Because all that came about was a sexual freedom, as opposed to a real dialogue. That sexual freedom supposedly equaled feminism.

BOWERS: It's so sad to be searching for sexual freedom at this point. That's how backwards we are. People are so uncomfortable with their bodies still. I think the market discourages feminist practices and political work in general. Modernism, abstraction ... it's all easier to sell.

OPIE: I don't have problems selling my most aestheticized work. But when I do tougher work—like the black-and-white *American Cities*, or even *Lesbian Domestic*—that work doesn't necessarily sell easily, but I don't really care. ... It's nice when you make money though. *(laughs)*

BOWERS: I usually think the work isn't good enough if it sells easily. For the last two years, when commercial transactions involving my work come up, I ask for a percentage of the sale, where it's applicable, to go to a nonprofit activist organization. I ask for equal financial commitment from the artist, collector and gallerist.

OPIE: How does that work, and do people really abide by those wishes of yours?

BOWERS: Well, the art market gives an obligatory 10-20% discount these days. When a collector asks for a discount I say, "sure," but I ask that the money go to a non-profit. It's never an easy negotiation, but some collectors are really enthusiastic about the idea.

OPIE: I think that's brilliant, I wish we could implement that with all the people that go through the UCLA studios trying to buy these young people's work. That they have to give a donation to UCLA to have access.

(laughter)

BOWERS: Yeah, I think the growth and proliferation of the art market has had a negative e ffect in the classroom.

OPIE: Wow, seriously. I mean, UCLA is ...

BOWERS: ... well, you're in the hotbed.

OPIE: I am in the hotbed. I'm in the get-outta-grad-school-get-a-gallery-and-become-famous ...

BOWERS: How does this affect your teaching?

OPIE: There was a beautiful article recently about Louise Bourgeois. It was an interview where she was talking about how she's so glad she didn't become a fa-mous artist when she was young, because she had all those years to develop her work, and that she feels really, really sorry for the young artists of today, because they don't have any time to develop their work. And now women, if you're in your 40s and you haven't had a solo show ...

BOWERS: There's very little interest.

OPIE: ... you're screwed. And a lot of my friends are facing that. I mean I know so many amazing artists and it's like ... they'll scoop somebody up, right out of my UCLA grad program, but God forbid they show these very developed artists, you know?

BOWERS: I admire how proactive you are in supporting other artists. Although there are many more opportunities for women artists today, the inequalities are still huge. There's still a glass ceiling, particularly in publishing. That's why I think it is so important that we are doing this interview together.

OPIE: Well, it's the same thing with me. I'm gonna have four floors at The Guggenheim ...

BOWERS: I mean, c'mon Cathy, I'm so happy for you!

OPIE: ... yeah, it's unbelievable. But at the same time, whenever one of my contemporaries—Wolfgang Tillmans, Jack Pierson—sneezes out a photograph, a book is published.

BOWERS: In the realm of art publishing, for every three publications on men, there's only one devoted to women. How many books have been published on your work? I know of three.

OPIE: I only have museum catalogues. I do not have one monograph. For what—how many bodies of work? How many images? And I've never had an article in Artforum—not once, ever.

BOWERS: Are you serious?

OPIE: Yes. Not that I think Artforum's the pinnacle.

BOWERS: In a book called, *After the Revolution: Women Who Transformed Contemporary Art*, they actually offer statistics that examine the number of solo exhibitions by women artists.[3] In the 1970s, women accounted for 11.6 percent of the solo shows and it rose to 23.9 percent in the 1990s. Since 2000, the percentage has dropped to 21.5 percent. On average, group shows contain no more that 18 percent women artists. What are the percentages like in your classrooms?

OPIE: Sometimes I only have one man in the class and the rest are women.

BOWERS: Exactly.

(laughter).

I mean, you can't tell me all these women quit making art after graduate school or that their works are inadequate, or of lesser quality than their male counterparts.

3 Eleanor Heartney, Helaine Posner, Nancy Princenthal, and Sue Scott, *After the Revolution: Women Who Transformed Contemporary Art* (New York: Prestel, 2007)

OPIE: No, no—of course not. Well, let's go back. I want to go back to a question that I had when you were talking about feminism and the young students' approach to it. Do you think—and this is true idealism —but do you think that the *Wack!* or *Multiple Vantage Points* exhibitions are going to change some of the younger artists that we teach? Do you think that these shows are actually gonna open up their minds in certain ways?[4]

BOWERS: I'm optimistic. When I was young, I saw a show about process art that completely changed my practice. The human scale of the work, the accessibility of the content, and the celebration of process that I learned from that show still effects my practice today. It's hard for me to be objective about *Wack!*'s impact because during the time of these feminist exhibitions, I was teaching at CalArts, and I think it is no coincidence that I was hired as the visiting artist during this time period. My interest in feminism could be a bridge between these exhibitions and the academic environment.

OPIE: Right.

BOWERS: This teaching experience was a tremendous gift. I have never worked in one school with such a powerful group of young artists who embraced feminism.

4 *Wack! Art and the Feminist Revolution*, curated by Connie Butler, The Museum of Contemporary Art, Los Angeles, The Geffen Contemporary, March 4 - July 16, 2007
Multiple Vantage Points: Southern California Women Artists, 1980-2006, curated by Dextra Frankel, Los Angeles Municipal Gallery–Barnsdall, Febryary 25th - April 15th, 2007

Although mainly women, this group included men as well. They organized a feminist conference and feminist exhibition around the *Wack!* show. I can name ten women from that program who are kickass artists making work dealing with contemporary feminist issues.

OPIE: But CalArts also has a whole history of a feminist art program.

BOWERS: It's no accident. These are institutional ideological decisions. The faculties select the type of young artists that will be in their programs. The agendas set by academic institutions have great influence upon the future direction of art practice.

OPIE: But ... the market still likes sexy. I never intended the queer portraits to be so sexy. Now they're sexy, but initially they weren't regarded as sexy. People were a little freaked out by them.

BOWERS: Not all your work is sexy, Cathy. *(laughs).*

OPIE: No, not all of it's sexy.

BOWERS: What the hell is "sexy" art? Can we get back to aesthetics?

OPIE: Yes, we can get back to aesthetics. I'm interested in beauty as a dialogue. Not in a Dave Hickeyesque dialogue. *(AB laughs).* But I'm interested in it, I come from a core belief that in order to get people to engage with work, they have to want to engage with it visually. And so I use all the classical tropes to do that. But, in the end, there's always something else. You know, it's like if you look over there at *Self Portrait Nursing*—it's the basic Madonna and child portrait—but it's of my child Oliver and I. He's nursing and, you know, I'm a 41-year-old woman in that photograph with "pervert" carved on my chest, and I'm completely tattooed up. An image like this has all these layers to it. If I just made this really intense, raw image that didn't necessarily use the classical tropes, I think that I wouldn't be as interested in it, visually. I mean, to me it would be like I'm trying to be rough, and I don't want that. It's like that whole thing where people thought I was mean.

BOWERS: Mmm-hmm.

OPIE: I don't want to be mean—I want to be thoughtful. In order to be thoughtful and to get people to think in a different way you have to, I feel, kind of seduce them a little bit with beauty.

BOWERS: I use aesthetics in a similar way in my work. You know, I'm not afraid of the term "propaganda" and there's no attempt at neutrality in my work. I want to make work that is conceptually driven and I take a political and activist position. These issues often divide people, so I use aesthetics as an entry point for viewers so they don't automatically react against the content. Instead, the aesthetics kind of seduce them into being willing to …

OPIE: … to sit with it.

BOWERS: … to sit with it.

OPIE:: To let it seep in.

BOWERS: Exactly.

OPIE: Well, it's what slogans do.

BOWERS: That's interesting. What do you mean?

OPIE: Such as Barbara Kruger's work. The slogan begins to create ideas that have a conceptual framework in their direct dialogue with both the work and with advertising. Because of the slogans, people react to the work, and are able to identify it as a recognizable platform.

BOWERS: I think you're talking about populism or accessibility, right? I like that analogy. I've always avoided thinking about my work in terms of slogans because of how quickly slogans are read and consumed. I want to reveal the complexities of the subjects I'm dealing with—something the media avoids. I'm a storyteller and I want to tell the whole story, not just give a sound bite. Artwork is a form that allows you the gift of time.

OPIE: Right …

BOWERS: Lately though, I've been questioning my use of aesthetics and looking at alternative strategies used by other artists. I've been thinking a lot about social and dialogical practices—artists that focus on the process of dialogue and collaboration, not the physical or formal qualities of an artwork.

The problem with that is that I find such joy in working with materials.

OPIE: I'm glad that you find joy in working with the material aspect of art and that you have solid ideas in relationship to those materials. It's important to be honest with yourself.

BOWERS: Well, besides being honest about my attachment to materiality, I have come to the realization that every project I choose starts with an emotional response to the subject matter. It's embarrassing to admit, but I will not start a project if I don't have a gut response to it. However, I think this type of emotional response is very different than sentimentality.

OPIE: But isn't that, in a corny kinda sense, what art is supposed to do, anyway?

BOWERS: Well, I don't know. I mean, that's why it's embarrassing for me to admit it.

OPIE: Sentimentality is a tricky word, but if used correctly it can evoke an amazing emotional response. Such as—I don't know if you ever walked through this installation, it's still one of my all-time favorite exhibitions I've ever seen in L.A—when Christian Boltanski did *Lessons of Darkness* at MoCA. I literally felt my body shift. I started thinking about how he uses sentimentality within his work to create that emotional response.

BOWERS: I really fear sentimentality and nostalgia. Because I think they can be, well, they erase the complexities of history. It's like looking backwards with rose-color-ed glasses.

OPIE: I don't know. ... Okay, let's look at these two photo-graphs on the wall. *(There are two new sets of images hanging in Cathy's studio. One set was taken at the Mayday immigration march in Los Angeles and the other comes from an anti-war protest march in Hollywood that marked the fourth anniversary of the start of the war.)* I mean, look at them. Nobody is really protesting. It's only out of nostalgia and sen-timentality toward an idea of democracy in America that these people are truly out there. However, in the immigration march, they really are protesting, and they're passionate within their action.

BOWERS: I participated in both marches. The immigration rally—the one where there was supposedly almost a million people downtown—was the most powerful march in which I have ever participated.

OPIE: No, that's protesting. In these peace-march photo-graphs, people are not protesting. Yes, they're car-rying coffins. But as they're carrying coffins, they're talking on cell phones.

BOWERS: Right. Well, they've gotta see if they're on TV, Cathy. They're calling home to see if they're on TV. *(laughs).*

OPIE: So, it's interesting to me, to think about, "Is it out of sentimentality and nostalgia that people are taking to the streets? Or is it out of truly thinking that they can create change in American culture?"

BOWERS: I actually think the war in Iraq isn't real enough for people yet. I think these are the people *(pointing at the anti-war march photos)* who are upset and feel an obligation to get out. But I think the American people have been distanced from the war through the corporate media, through the Bush administration. You know, ideas like, "Let's fight it over there, so we don't fight it here," the refusal to institute a draft, embedded reporters …

OPIE: … right.

BOWERS: The only people really experiencing this war are the military families. On 9-11 the president told the American people to go out and shop. *(laughs).* Right? This Administration has done an amazing job of not making this war personal. We all know that "the personal is political." People in military families experience this war firsthand, but the majority of Americans do not. The immigration battle, on the other hand, is real for many people in this country. The families and communities of undocumented immigrants experience it firsthand; they're not buffered. They experience the fear, the separation of families, and the ICE raids. They live in this country, they believe in this country, and this country is abusing their rights, don't you think?

OPIE: Mmm-hmm.

BOWERS: The war truly isn't personal to most Americans; it isn't affecting their lives—and that's what I think the difference is between the immigration protests and the war protests.

OPIE: That's interesting. And to me it is so personally sad —and maybe this is also steeped in nostalgia—that people really have this belief in America as a true democracy.

BOWERS: We are part of the "Me Generation." The focus on the self is more dominant that ever. I fear that the idea of the "personal as political" has been co-opted to mean self-interest, rather than a group-based identity.

OPIE: So much about each of our work comes out of a personal-is-political position.

BOWERS: Right. And I think that both of us are asking our viewers for empathy. Right now in this country, I see a cultural lack of empathy, or maybe of citizenry. Until it's personal, we don't get involved. Perhaps our positions are similar. I believe that protest is still a powerful force for change. I just think it requires the commitment of its members.

OPIE: Did you read Cindy Sheehan's letter?

BOWERS: Yeah. In fact, I was so touched by it.

OPIE: I remember the day the letter came out, and when I was reading it. And I was thinking about that kind of position—of the personal and political. And that Sheehan, you know, obviously had become political through the personal loss of her son in this war.

BOWERS: And tried everything to motivate others.

OPIE: And then, literally, she quit. Creating a letter of resignation to the American people ...

BOWERS: ... because she was broke and exhausted. And it wasn't the Republicans who failed her; it was the Democrats by continuing to fund the war.

OPIE: And I really believe that this is exactly what the anti-war protestors are feeling too. They're marching because they feel a responsibility to march, but they don't actually think that they can create change. And, you know, that is so profoundly sad to me.

BOWERS: There's a sense of desperation, because it feels like the actions of the protestors won't be recorded and their voices won't be heard—because the free press is in such peril. Protests are under-reported.

OPIE: We have no free press, and most of the blogs from the young soldiers in Iraq that were interesting have been shut down by the military.

BOWERS: Yeah. And the reason protest works is because it gets reported.

OPIE: Well, the idea that a certain number of people come out on a specific day throughout the country to protest the war is obviously better than if no one did. What motivated me to create these images was a sense of solidarity with the people and the protestors, in relationship to the possibilities of democracy, and that, the photograph in itself, would create a document ...

BOWERS: But it seems like something so hideous has to happen before the mainstream media reports it. Like with Katrina, in New Orleans.

OPIE: Oh, wow. The way the governmental agencies are handling that is still a joke.

BOWERS: So much was covered up. But it has to be that bad before the media is able to become outraged, despite that the poverty and inequity existed long before the hurricane.

OPIE: Mmm-hmm. But even that—the outrage didn't change anything.

BOWERS: But, Cathy, what the hell! We still have to keep fighting.

OPIE: Oh, I know ... we have to fight the good fight. I mean, I feel so bad for Cindy Sheehan having to write that letter of resignation. But writing that letter of resignation was also a completely political gesture.

BOWERS: I don't believe for a minute that she is really quitting. She will start a new organization, run for office, in some way, I am sure she will continue as an activist. At the time it was published, Sheehan's statement of resignation was profoundly depressing.

OPIE: I wept. How can you be a political artist? How can you be a political person in today's society? You can take to the streets, you can show it; you can talk about it; you can try to create work around it, but, at the same time, and at this point, you don't have the same kind of idealism that you had in your youth. You know that by creating work like this, it actually isn't going to do anything except to document a moment. And perhaps that in itself is okay for me now.

BOWERS: Cathy, I think it does more. I have more political agency now than I did in my youth. Perhaps I'm more optimistic than you because I wasn't as active when I was young. I think art can encourage others to speak out. I think it can inspire people—even if it just inspires artists. I also believe that art can have an effect on peoples' political philosophies, and that has to occur before their participation in activism. I also think that to document—to bear witness—is so important, because what you're doing—especially someone at your level of success—is creating images that become part of a museological archive. And it is so important to have images like these protestors hanging here in your studio, or the *Pervert* photo, or the lesbian domestic photos in our visual history rather than, say, a continuation of modernist abstraction.

OPIE: No, I agree with that. But, at the same time, you know, when I was in my 20s and my 30s, I was more idealistic that art could actually create change. And I really tried to function from that place. And maybe I made one less homophobe in the world—maybe I have—but I don't actually know that I have. In fact, I'm just watching our country become more and more homophobic. So it's hard to be idealistic.

BOWERS: I don't think I'm idealistic. This is all I can do because I so profoundly believe in the ideas I focus on in my work. This is where I must return to the importance of community. I may make work about the injustice of global systems, but it always comes from the perspective of small communities of people. All I can focus on is the impact of one small community's actions upon the belief systems and actions of other communities.

OPIE: Even though I say that it's hard to be an idealist, obviously both of us are idealistic in trying to create the recognition of a possibility of change within our work. By being passionate and by being engaged in our communities and the politics of those communities—I am going to have to agree with an earlier statement—I think you are right … that you can inspire people, and I suppose that little bit of gain, that's what compels me as an artist to explore the injustices within our culture.

BOWERS: And the beauty in our culture.

Andrea Bowers
The Weight of Relevance, 2007
3-channel video (color, sound, 26:15 min. looped)
DVDs, DVD players, synchronizer, video projectors, speakers, 80.5 x 435 inches
Installation view, Secession, Vienna. Photo: Christian Wachter

Catherine Opie
left: *Self Portrait/Nursing*, 2004
C-print, 40 x 32 inches
above: *Flipper, Tanya, Chole, & Harriet, San Francisco, California*, 1995
chromogenic print, 40 x 50 inches

Andrea Bowers
Stills from *Vows (Goldman, Emma. "Marriage and Love." New York: Mother Earth Publishing Association, 1910.)*, 2006
Two-channel video (color, sound; 21:07 min. looped)
DVDs, DVD players, projectors, two screens, synchronizer, speakers

Andrea Bowers
Stills from *Letters to an Army of Three*, 2005
Video, color; English version 55:35 min., Spanish version 55:54 min., looped

Catherine Opie
top: *Untitled #1 (Wall Street)*, 2001
IRIS print, 16 x 41 inches
bottom: *Untitled #5 (Wall Street)*, 2001
IRIS print, 16 x 41 inches
right: *Untitled #5 (Surfers)*, 2003
C-print, 51 1/4 x 41 1/8 inches

Catherine Opie
left: *Stolen red converses, in front of my house*, 2005
C-print, image size 16 x 20 inches
above: *Kristopher & Clara, Tulsa, Oklahoma*, 1998
Chromogenic print, 40 x 50 inches

Andrea Bowers
stills from *Sanctuary*, 2007
16mm color film, silent; 6:43 min. looped

Andrea Bowers images courtesay Susanne Vielmetter Los Angeles Projects.
Catherine Opie images courtesy Regen Projects, Los Angeles.

ISBN 0-923183-44-2 / 978-0-923183-44-8

This publication was made possible in part by the generous support of the
Peter Norton Family Foundation, the Foundation for Contemporary Art, and
the Norma Bartman Foundation.

Special thanks for the help of Annie Buckley editing, Fiona Jack editing and
transcribing, and Julia Brown copyediting.

Printed in Canada by Westcan.

Art Resources Transfer, Inc. is a nonprofit, tax exempt organization
dedicated to establishing a more egalitarian access to the arts
through publishing (A.R.T. Press) and the free distribution of
books to public libraries and schools in underserved communities
nationwide (D.U.C. Program).

Between Artists is a series of conversation based books that
document different positions and strategies of contemporary,
critical visual practice. These conversations provide an opportunity
for artists to speak clearly about their practice and give readers a
better understanding of the power and relevance of the artists'
voice in the discussion of larger social issues.

www.artresourcestransfer.org

Series edited by Alejandro Cesarco
Copyedited by Wendy Tronrud